To Beth, with a garden of gratitude for our friendship. —M.S.
To my favorite biologist, again. —B.G.

A special thank you to Kaitlin Haase, Southwest Pollinator Conservation Specialist with the Xerces Society, for your expert guidance and all you do educate the community on ways to help pollinators thrive.

Copyright © 2026 by Michelle Schaub
Illustrations © 2026 by Blanca Gómez

All rights reserved
Printed in China
First Edition

For information about permission to reproduce selections from this book, write to Permissions, W. W. Norton & Company, Inc., 500 Fifth Avenue, New York, NY 10110

For information about special discounts for bulk purchases, please contact W. W. Norton Special Sales at specialsales@wwnorton.com or 800-233-4830

Manufacturing by RRD Asia
Book design by Hana Anouk Nakamura
Production manager: Delaney Adams

ISBN: 978-1-324-08211-8

W. W. Norton & Company, Inc.
500 Fifth Avenue, New York, NY 10110
www.wwnorton.com

W. W. Norton & Company Ltd.
15 Carlisle Street, London W1D 3BS

Authorized EU representative: EAS,
Mustamäe tee 50 10621 Tallinn, Estonia

1 2 3 4 5 6 7 8 9 0

Michelle Schaub

Illustrated by
Blanca Gómez

A Pathway for Pollinators

Norton Young Readers
An Imprint of W. W. Norton & Company
Independent Publishers Since 1923

Flitter.
Flutter.
Buzz.
Hum.

Come . . .

watch a meadow thrum.
See it sing
with flowers
and wings.

In this untamed, open space
pollinators
sip their fill,
toting pollen
from blossom
to blossom,

UNTIL . . .

the meadow ends
in steel and stone,
concrete roads,
neatly trimmed lawns of green.

Not much nectar in this scene.

As cities grow, meadows go.

Where will pollinators feed?
Can we give them what they need?

Connect
one wild place
to the next.
Habitats linked
dot to dot.
A chain of pollinator pit stops.

Ready to start? Let's find some land. . . .

Larger spaces would be grand.

What to look for?
Vacant lots,
or boulevards;
below the rows of power lines.

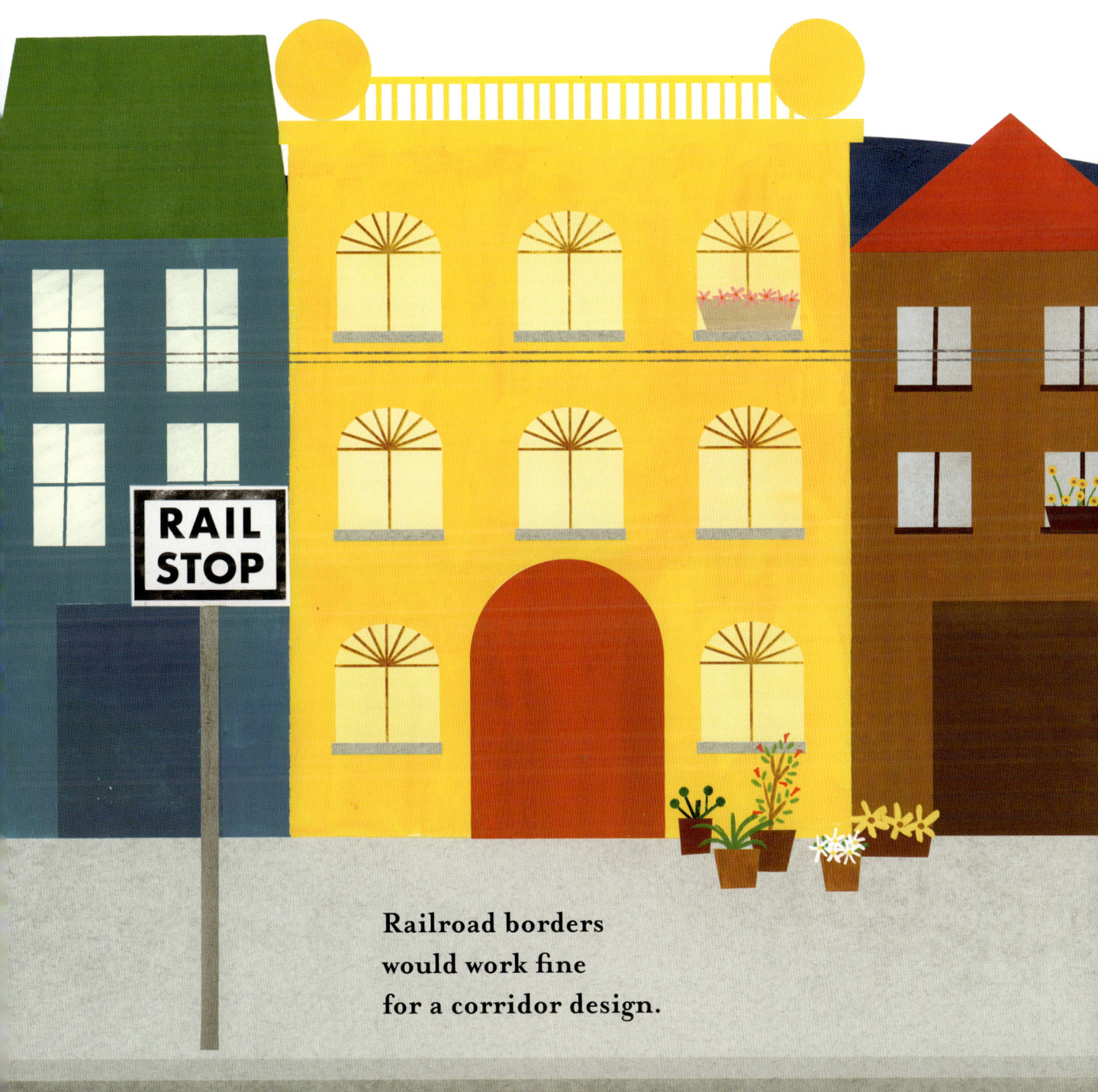

Railroad borders
would work fine
for a corridor design.

No large plots?
Well, smaller spots
are vital too.

A window-box oasis,
a rooftop with a view,
the corner of a balcony. . . .

A patch of yard will do
for pollinators passing through.

Now time to plant . . .

some BLOOMS.

Choose native ones that range in size and hue and shape, each flower matched to different pollinators' traits. A pollen-nectar smorgasbord!

Help them grow . . .

all season long
to keep the pollinators strong.
A steady supply,
day by day . . .

and through the night.
That's right!
Some pollinators feed
under evening skies.
For nocturnal flights,
grow flowers that shine
in pale moonlight.

All set? Not quite.

If there's room
amid the blooms,
add nooks and crannies,
shrubs and trees,
where visitors can rest
or make a winter nest.

Remember that it's best . . .

to be mindful
with the spots we tend.
Avoid the use
of chemicals
that harm our fragile friends.

When we give pollinators what they need,
they help grow plants,
grow fruit,
grow seeds,

and nurture Earth's diversity.

Flitter.
Flutter.
Buzz.
Hum.

Come. . . .

Build a pathway.
Watch it thrum,
to welcome pollinators,

and everyone!

WE NEED POLLINATORS

What are pollinators? They're the bees, butterflies, birds, bats, and other animals that visit flowering plants and trees to feed on nectar and pollen. As pollinators feed, pollen, a powder that contains the plant's reproductive cells, sticks to their bodies. When they move to another plant of the same species, that pollen brushes off, fertilizing the plant and enabling it to produce fruits, seeds, and new plants.

Without pollinators, we would have a hard time feeding ourselves. Over 80 percent of all flowering plants depend on pollinators to reproduce. One out of every three bites of food you eat exists thanks to pollinators.

POLLINATORS NEED US

Like people, pollinators need food, water, shelter, and space for populations to flourish. Unfortunately, pollinators around the world are in decline. One reason for this decline is loss of habitat. Meadows and other wild places have been replaced with cities, towns, and farms. Isolated parks and preserves do not provide enough space for pollinator populations to thrive.

One way to help pollinators is to provide more sources of flowering trees and plants. Pollinator-friendly gardens have been around for some time. But what if individual gardens and other landscapes could work *together* to revive the health of pollinators? That's the idea behind **pollinator pathways**.

A NETWORK OF PIT STOPS

Pollinator pathways are clusters of native plants that provide food and habitat and are close enough to one another to be within the traveling range of most local, native pollinators. These "pit stops" form a safe and nutritious pathway for pollinators. For example, many native bees have a flight range of about 150 meters, almost the length of one and a half soccer fields. If pollinator gardens are planted within a 150-meter radius of one another, those bees can travel between them and reach the food they need. Pollinator pathways help reverse habitat loss.

Sections of a pathway can stretch several miles along railroad tracks, or be as small as a window box. The best pollinator pathways are a community effort, involving local governments, businesses, schools, libraries, clubs, and individuals in the effort to create a connected habitat for pollinators.

When it comes to pollinators, every hand (and flower) helps.

POLLINATOR-PLANT MATCHUP

It's important to choose the right blooms for a pollinator garden. Many pollinators depend on specific plants. A good example of this is the monarch butterfly. Monarch caterpillars only eat milkweed plants. They need milkweed to grow into butterflies.

To select the best plants, learn what pollinators live near you. Then choose native plants that those pollinators use. Native plants are well adapted to local climates and soils. Once established, these tough plants are easy to care for and rarely need to be watered.

Arrange your plants in clusters. Pollinators are more likely to notice a group of plants versus a single plant. Be sure to choose flowers that bloom at different times of the growing season. Different pollinators are active at different times of year. A diversity of plants will support a diversity of pollinators.

PLEDGE TO BE PESTICIDE FREE

Pollinators are fragile creatures. Pesticides, harsh chemicals that kill unwanted plant and animal pests, are harmful to pollinator health. To provide a safe space for pollinators, protect them by not using pesticides in outdoor spaces.

NOOKS AND CRANNIES, PLEASE

If you have the space, add a shrub or tree to your pollinator garden. Many trees and shrubs grow flowers that provide an important food source for pollinators. In addition, the nooks in these woody species make excellent shelters. Leaves and fallen branches provide nesting materials for pollinators. In winter, stubble from plant stems provides cozy crannies too.

On a balcony or rooftop, along a boulevard or railway line, dot-by-dot these gardens form a chain for pollinators to follow from one stop to the next. They also create beautiful places for people to enjoy.

Plant your own pit stop and be part of the pathway to pollinator health!

For more information on pollinators and pollinator conservation, visit:
https://xerces.org/pollinator-conservation